Praise for Trotting Race of Time

Rich Furman's remarkable collection of poetry, *Trotting the Race of Time*, summons up in riveting detail a Mexico and Central America marked by poverty and violence. The immersive poems document encounters with children, soldiers, candy sellers, revolutionaries, mothers, and fieldworkers-turned-killers in haunting lines, their humanity illuminated by Furman's compassionate eye. The dreams and sorrows of the late twentieth century here shine and grab the reader as relevant as ever, a source of current trouble and hope.
~ Kathryn Rhett, MFA, Professor of English at Gettysburg College, poet and nonfiction writer, author of *Immortal Village*, *Souvenir*, and *Near Breathing*

Trotting Race of Time is transformative poetry at its finest—work that goes straight to the heart.
~ Nicholas F. Mazza, PhD, Editor, *Journal of Poetry Therapy*, President, National Association for Poetry Therapy, Dean and Patricia V. Vance Professor Emeritus, Social Work, Florida State University

In *Trotting Race of Time* Rich Furman demonstrates his mastery of the narrative form—poems that traverse, narrate, and reflect. His deft language and imagery crackle. To perform these acts of witness that are so important, especially during this cultural moment, Furman and his poems "reach down into words as seeds of living."
~ Jack Martin, MFA, recipient of the Colorado Council on the Arts Poetry Award. Martin's works have appeared in *Agni*, *Another Chicago Magazine*, *Black Warrior Review*, *Crazyhorse*, *Diagram*, *The Midwest Quarterly*, *Ploughshares*, *River Styx*, *Quarterly West*, and many other magazines.

The poems that comprise *Trotting Race of Time* illuminate truths seemingly impossible to capture. The author's daring lyricism gives the reader no choice but to travel by his side, suffer in the blister heat, and wonder.
~ Roger Roffman, PhD, Author of *Marijuana Nation* (Pegasus, Books)

Are words, images, and ideas irresistible? Rich Furman answers this query with a bold "yes." No ordinary compilation—poems that lure you, draw you toward a Central America you must meet.
~ Peter Szto, Ph.D. Arts-based researcher, Professor of Social Work, University of Nebraska Omaha

Trotting Race of Time

Rich Furman

Colorado Springs, CO
www.universityprofessorspress.com

Book Copyright © 2020

Trotting Race of Time
By Rich Furman

All rights reserved. No portion of this book may be reproduced by any process or technique without the express written consent of the publisher.

First Published in 2020, University Professors Press.

ISBN: 978-1-939686-61-9 (print)
ISBN: 978-1-939686-62-6 (ebook)

University Professors Press
Colorado Springs, CO
www.universityprofessorspress.com

Front Cover Art by Marguerite Laing
Cover Design by Laura Ross

About the Cover Artist

Marguerite Laing was born in Auckland, the great granddaughter of one of New Zealand's most esteemed artists, Charles Blomfield. In the 1970s, while living in London, she met and later married the eminent Scottish psychiatrist and author, R.D. Laing. When not in London, they spent their time in the enchanted mountains of continental Europe and the United States with their son, Charles, until Laing's death in 1989. For more than two decades Marguerite has had a psychotherapy practice that imparts some of her work with an other-worldliness, sometimes inspiring an artistically profound sense of human experience. There is a poignant serenity in much of the work; in others, a sense of communion, some might evoke transcendence, a glimpse into the eternal present moment. Many of Marguerite's original works are held in private collections in London, Rome, California, Colorado, Singapore, Tokyo, Sydney, and Auckland. The University of Glasgow's Special Collections Department holds 35 of her originals from her years with Laing.

Table of Contents

Dedication	i
Introduction	iii
Part 1	**1**
84 Days	3
The Border	5
La Frontera	6
San Simón	7
Of Eyes and Mouth	8
Juanita	9
Qué Qué	10
The Fields	11
Watch Out Below	12
Help for the Helpless	13
Renovation	14
And We Are Gone	16
Damp Calls in the Air	17
To the Center	18
What Is Needed	19
Lying in Wait	20
Snap	21
Advice from Rats	22
Tegucigalpa, Honduras	23
Alone	24
Through the Wicked Plain	25
Remember	26
And We Are Right	27
Longing	28
Day by Day	29
We Supply the Dead	30
Aquí No Se Rinde Nadie	31
Dared to Dream	33

Nicaragua Libre	34
The Cheating Grip	36
For You	37

Part 2 — 39

Of Towering Walls	41
Falling South	42
You Can	44
Men	45
Trotting Race of Time	46
Peeling Posters, Patzcuaro	47
Morning in Morelia	48
Always Too Much	49
Sometimes All You Can Do Is Ride Death to the End and Hope She Lets You Off	50
With Each Movement	51
Revolution Monument	52
Of Conquests Dreamt	53
The Same	54
The Next Open Door	55
Trolls	56
Strange Solutions to Our Lack of Acceptance of Our Developmental Stage	57
Another Chance	58
La Zona Rosa	59
T-Shirts on Local Men	60
Por Qué	61
Mercado de la Revolución	62
El Tule	63
Mummies	65
Credits	67
Author Biography	69

To Hammie

You are not a good boy. You are the best boy.

Introduction

The backdrop of these poems is the complex and painful relationship between the United States and the nations of Central America as it played out in the mid to late 1980s. This brief forward can in no way address the complexity of the times, but a brief exploration may help readers make sense of some of the dilemmas that I encountered. It is also my hope that many of the poems are able to transcend the geopolitical moment in which they were written and stimulate personal self-reflection. It is my interest in self-reflection, meaning making, authenticity, and personal agency that, I believe, led Louis Hoffman, one of the founding editors of University Professors Press, to reach out to me about publishing my work.

Writing has long been the primary way that I make sense of my life and my main vehicle for growth and healing. While I have always been a student of language and craft, my career has been largely defined by my explorations of the functions of poetry and writing beyond their artistic merits. Most of the poems found in this volume were written more than five years prior to my discovering the discipline of poetry therapy. I would not begin to develop arts-based research methods using poetry for nearly another decade, yet in the poems found in this book lie some of my earliest attempts to explore poetry not only as art, but as therapy and social research.

Most of these poems were written within a year of the ten months I spent traveling throughout Mexico and Central America in 1986 and 1987. Editing poetry written over thirty years ago is a fundamentally fraught task. I have been tempted to extensively rewrite many of these poems, as my own aesthetic sensibilities and skills have changed markedly over the decades. However, since this is not solely a book of literature, but a poetic exploration of my own personal growth and development, I have kept my editorial touch as light as possible. Also, while my original layout of the manuscript had been chronological, I have elected to flip the chronological order of the two sections. The poems written in and about Nicaragua, Guatemala, and Honduras now appear prior to those situated in Mexico. The Central American-focused pieces seem like the stronger poems to me today—more complex perhaps, and more deeply situated within the social context of the time—and so there I begin.

I am humbled by and grateful for Louis Hoffman's interest in my poetry and scholarship. I had long given up publishing *Trotting Race of Time* as a book, and many of the poems found here had been published decades ago in small, print, literary magazines that no longer exist. *Trotting Race of Time* had been a finalist for several poetry book contests in the early 2000s—and I had given up after the fourth or fifth of these near successes. The book being published by University Professors Press—a small press that focuses on powerful works in humanistic and existential psychology, along with poetry focused on growth, change, and transformation—deeply warms my heart.

***

In the spring of 1986 I was studying photography in San Francisco, hoping to become a photo essayist. To pay the bills, I assisted studio photographers and worked in a graphics art house as a laminator—"Lamo Man," as I called myself. I lived a dual life: the one of an artist, and the one of fledgling activist protesting America's deadly involvement in Central America. For the previous couple of years, I had become somewhat preoccupied, haunted even, by the state-supported violence that ravaged El Salvador and Guatemala. It had become extremely hard for me to ignore a painful truth: The United States had trained terrorists at the School of the Americas in Fort Benning, Georgia, and was financing the torture and killing of hundreds of thousands of poor throughout Central America.

In the early 1980s, over a million people fled government-backed death squads in Guatemala and El Salvador. Throughout Latin America, millions upon millions of people disappeared from their homes and communities. Those who disappeared became just that—*los desaparecidos*, a term that haunts the nightmares of millions to this day. Many who were not killed risked their lives to escape the death squads and fled to the United States, leaving behind their communities, families, and lives. I met dozens of these brave souls when I volunteered in the sanctuary movement—a network of nonprofit and faith-based organizations that provided refuge and care for these unwitting pawns of the Cold War.

In January of 1986, I decided that a career in fine art photography was going to have to wait. I needed to step my toes across the small, abused isthmus of Central America. It was my intention to photograph the Contra War, to document the atrocities that United States' dollars were supporting. My plans changed as I began to volunteer at a hospital for abandoned children and discarded, disabled adults in Antigua, Guatemala. My heart was touched by several of the residents, and I began to question my career path.

After living in Antigua for six months, I took a month-long break from my volunteer work at the hospital there and traveled to Nicaragua to see the revolution. The Nicaraguan revolution had become a symbol of hope for young progressives and represented one of the few victories, temporary as it was, in the fight against the repression and imperialism of the Reagan administration and its covert wars. While there, I spent many hours getting to know poets and revolutionaries, as well as expatriates fighting against the crushing weight of American imperialism. I volunteered in a couple of development projects and construction brigades. I traveled. I thought. I wrote. I felt hope.

So much of my life had begun to change: my volunteer work, my writing. I knew that I would not return to photography. I had a vague sense that my future would focus on being of service and on writing, but I had no idea how these would come together. These poems document some of my early attempts at integrating these two selves. I hope reading these poems feeds your own desires for growth, healing, integration, writing, art, and witness.

Part 1

84 Days

84 days
from hell to hell
from death squads'
black hand neverness

to liberty's branding cattle prod
blue suits and steel
safeguard the indelible line
between us and them

between our separate
forms of misery

84 days
from Huehuetenango

its streets of indigenous brightness
markets of peppers screaming
campesinos working Shangri-La
emerald hillsides of coffee

to Los Angeles
pools filled with rocky dreams
air thick enough
to roller skate on
shattered hopes
stuffed into working sacks of denial

84 days
to walk they said
across the frontier
of the disappeared
where greening genitals
were stuffed into mouths
that could not confess
fast enough by roadside's rotting heat

across the Sierra Madres
where Guatemalan bones
turn to Mexican earth

to Tijuana's human coyote
rivers polluted with death
children with no arms
drinking in next generation
of children with no arms
or worse

it took you five days
and with your plastic freedom
six hours back

now in front of silicon
wondering how
you will rationalize this one

The Border

When you cross that mile stretch
of brown sterile earth
lifeless save for yucca and anorexic dogs

when your mind flips between visions
of Mayan mystical gurus
that might heal your sickest seeds
and the desolation that shifts under your feet
the desolation of everything you left behind

between photographs of the death squad disappeared
black bars over cigarette burnt eyes
and eternal volcanic cones
reaching towards a point of pureness
that doesn't seem to exist below

and each step brings you further
from what you imagined was you
and closer to what you prayed wasn't

your passport clutched
like a life vest to your chest
your shots, visas, traveler's checks
don't prepare you
for confronting emptiness
as you approach the hill

towards the border
Mexican blues becoming Guatemalan vapor

the dirt covers your shoes
your shoes are your heart
you clutch your traveler's checks
it doesn't seem to help

La Frontera

an arid brown shack
a pale dirt road
crab grass
scrub brush
two portly border guards
swatting flies
in the blistering heat
minutes past sunrise
a seal on documents
and half-hearted well wishes
trudging feet traverse
dust and fissures
money changers
are not shaman
and south
merely a direction
and the syllables
of Japanese tourists
trying to pronounce
Huehuetenango
and rickety school buses
with mufflers like vapor
filled with farmers
ambling towards their fields
and time
fading into the isthmus
like a chewable aspirin
stuck in a crying child's throat.

San Simón

They bring offerings of roasted chicken and grain liquor,
cigars and cigarettes, to the saint so human, viceful and failed.
Drop to their knees, ask for miracles for their sick or dying,
relief from card game debt or to sway fantasy love heart.

From his decaying wooden throne above, black tuxedo, plastic wry grin,
granting wishes for sinners who can do no right.
These are the ones he favors, derelict beloved saint,
part Mayan, part Catholic, Guatemalan holy mutt.

He is shared by all, the parish priest in conforming red robe,
the Quiché holy men outside,
their swaying supplication
and burning mirth and fires flailing to the above.

This isthmus rebels and is repelled, trampled by Yankee giants,
the Spanish armored knights, the moguls of dollar bitter fruit,
dictator death squads, failed coup after failed coup.
Bring lean pork and smooth rum to the wicked saint,
who quietly conjures his magic, the other saints long fast asleep.

Of Eyes and Mouth

Pastel wood benches just too short for American legs.
Lard cooked beans and tortillas made of blue corn and ancient hands.
Water, sugar and instant coffee mixed—the best is exported north.
Shove the dull liquid away from your plate. It nearly ruins the moment.
You read the local paper as young girls watch.
Innocent giggles accent words barely understood.
You look up into their eyes, and they turn away.
It is not fair to gift a five-child fisherman a tea strainer for a net,
the winds become embarrassed if seen for too long,
colonial ruins blush from exposure to mountain mist.
You ask for more tortillas, a little more chili to burn the lips,
feel the sting spread down your tongue.
Breathe deep to cool the fire that will not yield.
You roll another tortilla slowly, finish the liquid of your beans,
more chili to remind you of who you are.
You pay, leave behind the burn of eyes and mouths.

Juanita

I was barely not a boy when you called
me father, papa *en Español*.

You, Juanita, stricken with polio,
your face drooping left, limbs fissile, useless

dangling to sides like discarded threads,
or the child you were, dismissed for frailty.

Each day I came to visit,
you screamed for me shrill, eyes

boundless, head thrust back, tilted uncontrollable.
I held your feather light flimsy body, contorted arms locked in mine,

we slowly walked tortured laps around decaying courtyard garden
of the hospital that is your lifelong home.

Fed you each day for months
each bite you choked down

a painful victory followed by relief,
and a reminder of the cruelties of existence.

Never spoke of the future
we both knew all too well,

that when it would be time for me to return, you would think I,
like the others, left because of you.

Qué Qué

Alone in the gray soft shadows
the scowl of haunted caverns,

arms crossed silent,
and what nine-year-olds

fold their arms in such rage, but those
abandoned along deathsome roadsides,

or in shanty shacks, baking alone?
She waits for voices hurled between fragile ears,

her only communication an utterance or
maybe it's a word. No one really knows.

Qué qué, what what, does she intend
her yearning calls to compel us to know?

She follows me around the courtyard
and tilts her head to her shoulder whispering, *qué qué*,

what, what, phonics and eyes begging us to not fail.
I wonder how come not, *why why*?

Perhaps not yet ready,
never ready

to comprehend the reasons
for being thrown away

like littered, scavenged bones
to the scrap heap.

The Fields

Bare hands bent from years of seasonal work,
bananas here in the lowland swelter,
wooden huts with oil drum roofs,
dirt floors and flimsy walls for as many as can fit.
The fields leak poison, banned sanely in antiseptic north.
The ground oozes death, scorching toes, bones, days,
scratches the throat until silence.
One hundred twenty degree heat lulled only during lunch,
bought from the store the company owns,
for many times the cost, canned governmental provisions
from north, rent paid that sweeps away to someplace
called New York, some strange epic twisted nightmare.

***

He saves banana stickers as family death crests.
They remind him of his fourteen hour days in the banana fields.
That was before the day he was traded by chance, when he moved
to the city and learned to kill. It is easy work.
He rides with a few others, some trained in terror
in Fort Benning, Georgia, in secret sessions in dense woods.
They find the one marked,
remove him from his home, rape his wife if sweet.
In the car, they ram objects into him,
or break limbs, or slice unreplaceable, unspeakable parts.
Away from the city, they cut off parts completely,
stuff them into the mouth, leave the offender rotting by the road
with a white glove over his eyes so all would know.
It is easier than the fields.

Watch Out Below

The trees covered with green vines
form ladder steps of jungle dreams.

You climb to the roof of the jungle, the ceiling
of the universe, it seemed.

Each careful stop taking you out of yourself,
into the void you have forgotten.

Parrots bright flapping emeralds fly by
as common as pigeons,
monkeys with lions' roars
as frequent as city dogs.

The tops of the palms form a bushy horizon
extending forever.

There are no desk jobs up here
no fast food burgers
or Styrofoam flavored coffee.

No artificial flavored life
or add water and mix existence.

No need for thought
or fantasy.

The call of humans below imploring me to descend
sounds insane.

The siren of reason
casts death hand long shadows
masking the face
of what really is.

Help for the Helpless

Shaking with fear alone with your
compañeros the rats who share your wooly blankets
like stuffed animals by your childhood legs
playing pool with killers on tilted worn tables
who mistrust your green eyes watch you closely
such eyes only are owned by devils they say
the towering patchwork volcano in the distance also mistrusts
with its ancient steady patches of corn and crop so distant
yet beckon like the young women who strolled the streets together
show legs to tempt who wanted money not love
but need both in shanty shacks by edge of town existence
under the hot sun the gods tell you what to do
in Bahasa Indonesia you cannot read with bruised swollen hands
you study ancient language hope to learn soon
wait for clear messages watching the rats make love
the broken sewage pipe leaks a rhythmic beat down the wall.

Renovation

Mushroom selling mystics
trade round headed vision buttons
for greenbacks or sex.

Sand flies tear at your
flesh, tiny prehistoric gymnasts,
dancing on parts you never knew you had
in pressure cooker wetness and heat.

An old expatriate with eyes
the locals called demon eggs,
bangs rabid jumbled words
on an ancient typewriter of mourning.

Your hotel in the jungle,
through barking dogs miles,
shadowy palms casting nightmarish visions
across the white sand haunted roads.

Morning sky pounds you through
windows ten feet tall and wide
glassless save for jagged shards,
overlooking the pool filled with twisted metal and lumber,
where once tourists floated like spoiled red walruses,
with thick insulating hide to protect against
the wide eyed children's gapping stares.

In this three dollar a night wreckage
of this resort twenty years past dead,
you sift through another sort of ruins
also twenty years in the making.

A tedious renovation
of long hand filled notebooks,
silent hours gazing over the sea,
a placid yet angry tabula rasa
greening with projections
and agonizing agape lessons.

The buzzards fly side by side
with the seagulls, the dreams swiftly
following shifting sweaty nightmares.
When they become indistinguishable from one another,
from yourself, it will be time to go home.

And We Are Gone

Swing from hammock, the spray of tropical rain
colonial second floor porch, languid through time
below the white-washed ceiling and the plants that net
the sky ahead gray with glimpses of Caribbean light,
muddy streets, drenched soccer fans
returning from drunken canceled match,
dark, lean, in reggae dub celebrate
life, not rain or a game, each secondary to moment passing.
Store keeps cover open-air food stalls,
red beans, rice and salty fish stew in protected pots,
windblown rain sweeps away plastic covers they run to catch,
puddles form in seconds to overtake the potholed road.

She approached from behind gentle,
pleasant, plain, sweet vanilla.
Described the patterns of rain flailing as I stared ahead
closed my eyes to hear the words perfect:
the smells, the noise, the essence,
catching sideways glance of face never known,
not yet seen unimportant to words like river songs.

Later, alcohol mixed with grape juice wine from corner store,
and she was no longer plain.
Sweat room naked hands clutched.
Musk of days and nights, her smile, odor shrouds the room
lighting an embarrassed wanting glow.

When it was finished, she became plain again,
and this is how I fail often.
The morning came slowly, too few words,
and we walked with my bags to the docks,
felt her eyes watching, hoping,
wanting my lips to sculpt some words
like whittled carved wood in hands to save.
The ferry moving towards Belize, her figure
shrinking on the shore, in memories never made,
like a drunken fool stumbling down mountain pass,
I turn away to find a seat, and we are gone.

Damp Calls in the Air

The bending pole of the universe and the callous
song of the breeze, the trees above the sea, our
prison of Caribbean blue sky, leads us to the death
grip of post-industrial lostness. We lean back against
the timeless loft of lounge chairs and the
endless parade of visions, American dreams of bombs
away, watching the flecks in each other's eyes.
We are brothers under this horrible sun, as the
coconuts pound the beach like the war
in other innocent jungles, ruined by the markets of madness.
We open a package of bitter cheese, cover our bread:
there is little to do but this
attending to damp calls in the air.

To the Center

The green florescent lights
the smell of oily beans cooking
wave lazily through the window,
stained yellow tiles jet up from the floor
dangerous like barbwire, or rancid meat,
mildew lacing the tub a covered trail.
You take off your clothing
in front of the mirror.
A crack splits your body,
left to right,
past to present
soul to callous shell.
Holding your camera at your waist,
you snap discolored, distorted slides.
What else would these horrible
documents reveal.
A portal to the unseen,
to the insane rhythm of time
bending nauseous at the center?
You put on your pants, your shoes
the rest of it: the order of it all
seems predetermined as you sigh.
Walk into the streets, a dancer
facing west, forever towards the setting sun.

What Is Needed

The music was haunting.
The walls were thin and the
prostitutes moaned falsely of love,
naked concertos of boredom.
Outside, the dim cobblestone roads
were marked with the stains of silence.

All that was real was
merely a hologram you needed,
you turned to them, and they were gone.
It was what you discarded as senseless
that saved you.

You reach down tonight
into words as seeds of living.

Lying in Wait

I sit on this bench, filth,
outside the hotel, more filth
rent by the night, if I am paid.
Wait for men to want, not me,
but the skin, the flesh, the folds
they lie into, but do not touch,
my eyes to the ceiling and
mind other places. My body open,
things they never will force out, mine.
I will lie there and wait. They will finish.
They will dress quickly, our eyes will not meet.
They think about their wives,
or wonder about my health. I will wash.
I will scrub many times. I read in a magazine,
that if one touches you, their cells stay
with you for years. No matter, I will
scrape with rough soap and rinse. They will be gone, almost.
But not from my mind. Memories last
longer than sweet first kisses
I can hardly remember.
But for now, I will wait, and worse if they
do not come, do not tell me what they want,
do not pay me for what will sadden us both.
Worse to sit here painted, starched to the bench,
hours pass, the bones ache and muscles sore.
The boredom, is nearly as bad as the act.
Here comes one now. He asks me to use my mouth.
I will promise him this, but will only use my hand.
He may hit me, he may not. This one looks timid.
He will be scared of my distant gaze and wide-eyed smile, teeth.
He will leave quickly, like most of the rest.
He will not hit me. Christmas, only five months away.

Snap

I remember now of being
so frightfully alone,
that I would lie in the darkness,
count the ticks of the hotel clock,
that beat with the precision
of teenagers in the backs of first cars,
or the less steady beat under my chest,
and wondered, how many more
ticks or beats I could take,
before I would merely vanish,
without a witness
to even report of the event?
Three more beats, until I snapped
like an old fan belt?
But each day the sun would wake me,
and I would walk to the café
where the waitresses spoke more English
than I did Spanish.
They laughed, teased, called my eyes
huevos verdes del diablo:
green devil eggs,
and I would watch their breasts
move as they giggled,
and their giggles would feed me,
a nurturing soup to cure for moments
all that inflicted me.
After, I would roam the hillsides,
and the people would wave and stare,
and I wondered when
I would let myself go home.

Advice from Rats

The leaky roof pleased the cat sized rats,
that swim across the concrete floor.
They sing to you a sweet serenade of loneliness,
as you pretend to sleep,
pretend for whom,
you don't know.

You know nobody,
have nowhere to go.
Today's home, Comayaguela, Honduras,
a cheap motel where some come to die,
and other do anyhow.

Maybe your scurrying floor friends,
will tell you what to do.
You don't even have a clue.
You are thirty pounds lighter, diarrhea.
Your girlfriend died of shame.
Your friends died of confusion.

You have been dead,
four months now.
As the bedsprings push,
into the small of your back,
the prostitute from next door
swims to your bed to save you.

Tegucigalpa, Honduras

Is a bus cutting through the night,
rumble and exhaust spent and disregarded,

graffiti painted wall pleading and raging
for gringos to leave with their assassins and AIDS,

secluded airfield for cocaine and Contras
for slaving imports and murdering exports,

Comayaguela sex tour drunken madness for Marine advisors
the smell from the river and markets squabble shooting desperation,

dollar sign whore or a skinny dog limbless in the gutter squalor,
an abused child that wants no more,

the hopeless screams in the night echoed through walls in homeless hotels
and a stabbing that goes bad for both and a desert mirage flesh smelling.

Kafka without surreal metaphor, Hemingway without clean lines,
ice cream cone fallen to dirt with a bitter cherry dripping,

a deaf god in the face of desperate supplication,
a banana child with failure to thrive in bondless distance,
a scream of vocal cords cut, wavering through moonless night.

Alone

What do you do but beg?
Abandoned beneath the doorway,
face like the moon, beaten, alone?
The pastel colonial elegance.
The sway of lovely ignoring skirts.
The blistering sting. The shrapnel cuts. We are all alone.

Through the Wicked Plain

The frail alleys twisting like drunken sailors,
children kicking plastic water bottle along worn stone,
the clicking sounds, tap shoes on a lonely stage.

Legless lead eyes haunt the dark passageway up the valley walls,
balconies potted with bending flowers undulating in the wind,
the pastel yellow walls, the greening cemetery in the distance.

A worker stops to sip his water, the sweat from his brow
dripping off dark weathered skin, the moon retracting fast,
the day begins its march unrelenting through the wicked plain.

Remember

A plant silhouetted through
the tenement window
reflects our failure.

The dying blink of the neon sign,
the limp of dragging beggar,
the slow unconscious death cessation.

Tourists watch from behind safe rail,
flipping through guidebooks
searching for memories to be saved,
in basement stored postage stamps cut
from bills and letters they do not recall.

And We Are Right

The scent of mint,
trucks full of corn overstocked,

pyramids of wild herbs,
crates of smooth avocados.

Shadows, destiny waiting in the dark,
for the market gates to spring.

Slow trucks patched with tape and gauze,
drift down from the mountains.

We sit near some vendors,
their children draped in blankets,

herbs bundled with flowering skulls.
I comment on their beauty.

They tell us we do not understand.
They grow from the earth,

the spice tangy meats,
are merely life.

We smile at each other,
and we are right.

Longing

The pattering of memories light in their fade,
feet pulled lockstep through and dragging days

turned to weeks, months, the calendar a tumbling,
                                      spastic gymnast.

A sparse desk. Just enough space for a brittle, wooden chair,
between the lonely, narrow bed. The encroaching beggarly walls.

The chin fresh lines between the fingers,
patches of plaster watched for messages unfound.

It might be late summer. It might be next year.
The moments buoy a tumult, seas of the past

remember in the mornings, but never at night,
                              cruel, the twisting pang, a thorn
              of longing

Day by Day

The fifth day of diarrhea
sapped by emotions
worse than a leeching body
hoping to leave this Tegucigalpa hell.

You walk the streets
for the few fleeting moments of your strength
children play near pipes
carrying out the day's toxicity.

Day seven you pray to die
as cure seems as possible
as summer desert snow
with the rats you
make pacts written
in your blood

Whispers torment you
you hear them in your bones
like a ringing phone you cannot find
beans and tortillas still run though you
faster than the dropping flies.

Day ten hallucinations on the walls
faces drooling on your dismembered body
the mattress springs wrapping themselves
around your arms, legs, neck,
holding you still while the rats
sing songs to you about your death.

Day twelve there is a turn
food stays down, the fever breaks
feeling returns to your legs.
You pack up your things
ready to again begin life
Nicaragua a few hard miles ahead.

We Supply the Dead

They supply the weapons,
we supply the dead
        Salvadorian archbishop Rivera y Damas

Rusty crowbars pry
        marble smooth tires

recycling rubber each time
        to the less fortunate,

but still more so
        than some.

The death squads hold our hands
        and walk us across the road

to freedom. Lack of beans do not bother
        the rotting lips of traitors

and the less stomachs to be fed
        the less angry mouths to scream.

Summers have become peaceful
        here in the hillsides.

Aquí No Se Rinde Nadie

Just before crossing the border into Nicaragua,
fleeing from despair of

Honduran border town squalor of
teenage girls offering mouths and hands

for the cost of bread.
Our driver tell us his country

is no less a whore, the wretched in rags,
killed when inconvenient.

The bosses trade our children,
deadly jet fighters for coffee and beans.

More runways per square mile
than any land on earth,

transporting drugs and troops
and exporting any hope.

Coffee burned. Stinging bent fingers,
and then Nicaragua.

Dictator long banished, and when we crossed, his towering face,
painted on a sign, not a billboard for products

but the wide smiling peasant face of Sandino,
and words on mind like salt to open wound.

Aquí, no se rinde nadie,
Nobody gives up here.

A dignified promise from the lips of
daring smile, a threat beyond

the kindness firm. A face with eyes
that witnessed too much terror.

Determined words from those who bled deep
for centuries, like the time when

Somoza sold earthquake relief plasma
for a villa in Spain and slim hipped girls.

Basta, enough, and they were finished
and as we cross the dirt road marking the entrance,

the soldiers lifted us onto trucks,
whisking us south,

and we hoped that we
would not surrender either.

Dared to Dream

Forty nine dollars transformed to stacks of
flat faced revolutionaries long departed,
fresh soldier eyes study my face
study passport photo below
like memorizing a lover's face before protracted absence.

Trucks transported us to the capital, Managua,
westerners who will be interrogated back home
for *aiding and abetting* the enemy:
children playing barefoot soccer with trees for goals,
basketball on boiling cracked asphalt, netless bent hoops;
toothless dark farmers who share their penniless bread.

Weary exhilaration upon arrival,
find the supermarket for provisions.
boycott-induced aisles empty, save for finest Cuban rum,
block after block of twenty year post-quake rubble,
brown skirted legs, well rounded, wait for sweat packed bus,
revolution billboards proclaim the winners and losers
the saviors and saints, villains, liars and cads.

We swing from hammocks by day,
drink the rum, mixed with sharp tropical fruit,
at night, dance with revolution leaders, only
a few years our senior. Between songs and sways,
flirtations of worlds so far apart,
dangerous to the heart like fatty pork
we swayed and bent as the isthmus sailed
to a land that dared to dream.

Nicaragua Libre

Remember sleeping on a wooden plank
they called a bed,
each morning stiffer than death

my days in Nicaragua Libre,
wandering the countryside
more hope than I ever dared have,
more dreams than ever allowed.

And it was good, quiet enough
to hear my heart,
being just past twenty alone
sad but so alive so desperate
to find something real.

Holding others' triumphs so close
that I forgot they were not mine,
signing songs I barely understood,

borrowing heroes for the heat
the blistering swollen head,
walking miles under revolution's sky,
in truck rumbles on potholed roads,
soldiers passing me as I marched from
town to town they waved
sang danced shouted triumphs,

they seemed so much
younger, or maybe older
than I.

At night the parrots sang
teasing me with olive goddesses,
igniting my world aflame
it seemed eternal
time stood still,
for us to laugh

in the face of never,
to cry from merely
looking into the wind.

The Cheating Grip

The aisles were near bare
except for rows of Cuban rum
and at a dollar it was

the price of a meal or a hotel room,
smoother than Indian silk,
and we glowed in its aftermath,

and in the Managua sun, or the nuclear
fall we feared, away from the hunters of North,
amber shots to soothe the days unknown,

the swinging hammock shade
a bountiful basket to catch hazing visions.
The revolution was ending and

nobody dared utter a sound.
We had no guns
but days and time,

useless as philosophy to scarring livers,
dreams hid like the frail homeless on highway's edge
with a blind bus approaching and the wind

rattling the bones, chocking exhaust.
We became shadowy and discarded,
swimming fleshless skin in dark mole, and lone tortilla,

as the Contras maimed and murdered.
Soon it was north,
and all would feel cheated,

voices stuck in throats,
tracheotomy marks bearing down
on the cheating grip of drunken surgeons' hands.

For You

Your boots pound the stone hard
in spite of the care you take.
The narrow alley climbs above the town.
You are not meant to be here, away from the center,
the cafés, restaurants, places to buy, drink.
But the knife's edge feels soft to the skin,
the flimsy rocks crumble under feet,
the ones that will not stand the test of time.
At the top, children play mad laugh free,
They smile, as if only for you.

Part 2

Of Towering Walls

Looking down at your toiletry bag
it is easy to see that something is awry,
the priorities out of place,
as jumbled as partially beaten yolks,
but without their simplicity of purpose.

Your hands uncover the lies:
hair detangling formula,
organic avocado protein reinforced conditioner,
designer deodorant spray,
peppermint anti-plaque rinse.

Your floral tubes of chemically simulated life
do not mimic the essentials needed,
to stand the tests of time,
that which we can only guess,
but writing in the semi-dark with a nervous hand,
driving east on a two lane highway
just north of the border,
the burning road framed by cactus towering above,
shadows cast down in contorted form,
south of the angry black mountain,
under the shadow of Mexico's orange moon,
you begin to stab at the heart of such matter,
drench yourself in the fleeting blood
of moments such as these.
Trucks pass, anonymous wisps of blazing metal,
their drivers the same as the rest of us,
destined to travel in a familiar motion,
as hamsters in a labyrinth of towering walls.

Falling South

And then there was the hippie bus
no tobacco smoking the only rule.
Faded torn mattresses in place of seats,
passed beer and rum like water

we urinated down a funnel in the front
the liquid dodging the morning rush.
Connected with a failed lost pierced inked
body taken home for last American night,

left sheets soiled from game of sad pleasure
and I tried but could not even say goodbye.
The morning with friends, breakfast in Hollywood
with the actress/waitresses, director/busboys,

the smiles and schmoozing, the banter for a gig.
South through the traffic
we parked by the border, crossed,
found a liquor store for a quart

of almond flavored tequila,
stole sips in strip clubs and drank their cheap beer,
watched Marines stuff bills into G-strings,
suck old silicone breasts before they walked to the back

for drunken risky sex.
Then they brought out the donkey and a
sad faced teen mounted the beast.
This punctuated the end,
or the beginning of falling south.

Found a rooftop to sleep, passed-out overlooking
Tijuana's bars, the moon reflecting off
metal shacks, to the north the home
I would not see for many months.

Dreamt of white sand beaches, rich coconut meat
I would eat overlooking the sea. I opened my eyes south,
faced where the morning would take me, innocent like the
splayed fingers of a child reaching for the grip of loving warm hand.

You Can

Ponies shaved with stripes
painted as zebras for photo ops,
shellacked frogs on sticks
corn pipes in unfortunate mouths.

Designer jeans punched out in hilltop factories,
churning poison into streams and makeshift dumps
by small illegal hands
crippled by monotonous motion.

Old whore bars of silicon sadness
pander to sailors, drunken and free,
vagina mouths drinking cola to Bacchic roars
followed by donkey doll love play.

The waft of street vendor grilled meats
neon watts above flickering madness,
buses smog horns hide ancient rhythms
you can buy it all, you can

Men

Men hawking morning papers
don't care gringo sleep unknown.
Six a.m. tales cried in drunken madness
by the fountain that trickles brown water
into a basin of leaves and empty cartons.
The world's largest city cranks into gear,
an old muscle car careening downhill
through blind curves with burning brakes.
Invisible dogs in the market alone obsessed with meat,
the lonely awful task at hand.
Where is your god when the stomach rumbles,
the loins ache for touch?

Trotting Race of Time

Third class tickets do afford you a seat
on the night train from Mexicali to Mexico City.
Your sickness means little to those whose lives
depend upon the relief of a hardwood bench
covered with an inch of blue foam.

Airless, smoky cars are churning chicken coops
bellowing soot and steam,
sluggish chugging down the Sonora desert.
You hoist yourself onto the scalding roof,
anchor yourself with belt,
watch the sky, cactus pass like dark crippled gunslingers.

Discarded cars, deserted oil drums,
garbage bags piled to the sky.
Power plants spell progress to the poor,
unknowing effects of future fraud unspoken.

You scramble down quickly with the tunnel ahead,
hide between two boxcars,
feel the gut-wrenching rumble of the cars deep inside of you.
A young mother watches you through window,
gentle eyes yearn weary sad pity.

Sliding the door open, pushing past bodies asleep standing,
crammed into corner, the few awake stare shyly at burnt skin,
the conductor calls the next stop, shanty town mother ambles forward,
her form fading into abandoned waste, into the trotting race of time.

Peeling Posters, Pátzcuaro

the pastel decadence of a
cadence gone mad

slowed to the furious pitch
of the beating sun.

Morning in Morelia

He wakes each morning at three,
grinds fresh corn by hand,
rolls dozens of tamales,
salsa *roja, verde, dulce,*
queso y especial.

He places the fifty pound pot
on the rack of his bicycle
with the missing left pedal and slumping frame,
and rides down the mountain dark road
in the moonlight hiding the edge so near,
to take his place in the market.

In his faded torn shirt
American designer made in prior life,
the belt tightened to its final, yearning hole,
his hair slicked carefully to his scalp,
he calls his goods to the crowd,

to the bent old women shaping the perfect tortilla,
to the blind boy peeling fruit with razor knife
swirling around fingers like foam on high seas,
to the rib-wide sleeping dogs of shallow breath,
to each, faithful, purified, a monk behind monastery walls,
the results of prayer second to the faith, lonely words
called into the crisp forgotten air.

Always Too Much

Rusting metal ladders hanging from worn stone brick ledges
compete with the sun rising above gothic spires, the bells
that ring too rapid for the heart to bear.
The glare of orange blinding off the rusting doors.
A stop sign bent in half conceals intentions ignored
by the taxis and trucks leaving distant corners of Michoacán.
Men in white cowboy hats meet in the square and begin
stacking and folding newspapers in glacial perfection.
The singing birds begin to dissolve to the day
but for now, their cries in the trees, we pretend
not to hear, the cost of listening always too much.

Sometimes All You Can Do Is Ride Death to the End and Hope She Lets You Off

Psychotic fevers cannot be discarded
at one in the morning
into a lumpy bed in central Mexico
no matter how much you pray.
The rhythm of the marimbas
will not stop your agony.
You imagine lovers' screams howling through the walls
are phantoms of hate
that send you rolling on the floor
your body drenched in sweat
your mind roaming false to unknowable horrors
that descend into your room.
The shades flap violently above the window
the dancing ceiling fan marches towards you
like a parading monogrammed tombstone.
Weak and parched as the fever breaks
you open the door onto the courtyard,
your eyes strain to focus toward the sun,
children playing soccer shoeless and free,
you scratch your stomach,
feel your breath shallow but present,
run as fast as you are able to join them.

With Each Movement

He sweeps the square with a palm frond,
huge passes of the discarded,
through the dawn under the small church behind the market.
His method is perfect, each forward movement,
each pull, each shake to the side.
His face is still and strong.
He does not appear bored, to suffer from anxious excess.
He stands in the center, humming quietly a local hymn.
He is not thinking of his stock portfolio or
his new mobile wireless communication device.
He greets each pile, seems to thank them,
fills himself with each movement.

Revolution Monument

A kiss under Revolution Monument,
a moment stolen, hidden even from the dark.
You can hide among the twenty-five million
only if you are clever.
The collective eye watches,
a stern chaperone, a hawk searching for mice.
Watch over your shoulder even in pleasure.
The father who preaches discretion and chastity,
only for you to find a solid, hard-working man,
would shudder at this display of passion,
your skirt hiked, panties parted to the side.
The revolution has been won.

Of Conquests Dreamt

Mariachis lounge in the square,
haul horn cases and
fortify themselves with tongue tacos,
praying for five dollar gigs
to pay for rents back due.

Men peer over corral doors
as drag queens flirt and dance
with others who can pay for their drinks, for them.

Strip club neon lights flash unsteady,
hours sag, silent girls peer out the doors
to tempt with fantasy, so thinly veiled.

A mother holds her naked toddler and
points her vagina towards the street,
urine spouts forth, flows past the tourists,

who blind themselves, flip through guidebooks,
search for the next attraction to be crossed off their lists,
accountants of borrowed existence,
hash marks in the wooden beds of conquests dreamt.

The Same

The public filth obscures the fountain
in Buenavista square only for moments.

The falseness fades to the persistence of
the pounding daily afternoon torrent's crash,

a mother snapping Polaroids, a suffocating tuxedo
and white frilly lace unnaturally still,

a couple with guitars on laps, the fortune of youth
blind in songs, fighting the roar of the sky.

The green iron benches, the saggy palms, manicured poodles,
the pastel facades, the balcony garbage refusing to relent,

the baritone rumble bus, the stroking hair and laughter,
the hands that dance a mad language of love and lust,

the bronze statue watches the light shift to day's end,
tomorrow will be exactly the same, but completely different.

The Next Open Door

An amplifier strapped to his back,
he belts out blind songs of desire
in the subway for centavos.
His change cup held forward,
he waltzes down the crowded aisle smiling,
lips parted, his hands raised with the microphone
like an excommunicated lounge-act priest.

***

Selling candy for a peso is a rough way to go,
no one buying, car after car.
Awake at five to ride by six until midnight.
Why not grab a knife
and do things right?
But he belts his jingle in rhyming hawker song
the locals and tourists turn away, stare at their feet.
He leaves downtrodden, dead for some seconds,
rejuvenated as he walks though the next open door
to live small dreams that quickly fade.

Trolls

In front of the auto shop, the sign that reads,
multi-health services for your car,
the one-legged man in the Frankenstein rickshaw wheelchair,
begs for change in the center lane
of the highway that leads out of town.
He itches legs, real and missing,
the spot where the pant leg is sewn shut in cord and dirt,
the exhaust that coughs, the neglect from within their steel,
his hand trolls for change like a lure skimming the top of frozen pond.

Strange Solutions to Our Lack of Acceptance of Our Developmental Stage

You are passed on the roadside by a motorcycle.
The father in leather pants, boots, helmet.
His daughter in T-shirt, shorts, sandals, hair chasing the wind.
He enjoyed his time alone, and in the bar, before children.

Another Chance

Weed colored Beetles zip with no attention to lanes,
beggar digs cigarettes from between cracks
of beaten gothic brick, *machos* stroll and eye
señoritas with legs long and looks tired,
the towering church tilts to side like the head of perplexed dog,

like a defeated clown resting his painted face,
threadbare, frayed on elbow propped hands,
wishing for another chance, for another day
under the lights, and it's perfect.

La Zona Rosa

The begging children extend their empty paper cups between
the ropes of the outdoor café, toward the tequila-sipping gold-clad crowd,
they watch, all lips and laughter.
A wealthy man kicks a homeless dog rolled as a sad ball,
a cruel soccer practice of feet in leather and lizard,
Indigenous women sell dolls for next to nothing
by the dance club line, the lovely powdered faces,
legs posed just so, music, thumping, western,
electronic, the threads of her brilliant blouse frayed,
cyber cafés, padded couches and cappuccinos.

T-shirts on Local Men
or
Why Americans Are so Highly Regarded Abroad

Hooters University, New Jersey.
Pull my finger.
I found it and now my finger stinks.
I got shit-faced in Cancún.
Eat a pussy, save a mouse.
I'm with stupid and I happen to be alone.

Por Qué

We eat tacos and meats on the street
by the metro station market,
breaded meat *milanesa*,
tender flaky pork in green mole.
Suck on the bone to not miss a drop.
Breaded, dull colored beef,
tropical soda pink and pulpy.
The waitress, harried, smiling,
brings dishes out one by one,
slowly, for those who must learn to wait.
A begging couple enters,
the man's legs thinner than the bones on my plate,
head cocked to the side with eyes
pleading, seeming to expect indifference.
His shoes too large wagging like a truck's mud flaps.
We turn attention to tortillas
to soak up the last drops of sauce.
A guitar player strolls in full of songs,
sappy in any language. We give him some pesos,
finish our plates to the rumble of stomachs filled.

Mercado de la Revolución

Skin like the burlap sack
into which she folds
flowers, flowering herbs, a fragrance
reaching towards the ringing bells
like brass throated humming birds
from ancient ruined churches above
the corrugated metal market roof.

She hauls the bag, stuffed
larger than she, over her shoulders,
back, neck, head, eyes covered
by green jutting branches, buds.

She strains forward, begins
a march with short, steady steps,
yet quick and fluid as running water,
her arms wrapped around the sack
delicate thin like her flowers,
white cupped calla lilies,
sun-centered mums,
herbs so dark and green, almost black.

Thin, yet lasting,
like the plants she nurtures,
that nurture her,
that she places to her lips
the kiss of the mother.
She turns a corner,
lost to all eyes,
takes her place in the palace of time.

El Tule

Hitched ride in half packed hippie van
shoved between stoned lip pierced teen,
and bags of woven wonders to be hawked.
Through dusty roads green north Guatemala,
across machine gun guarded border,
kid soldiers with eyes of black flashed wide
for Yanqui smiles passing innocent and free.
We cross the border into Mexico,
suspicious brown hands explore with care.
Tired from months of travel we seek
el Notre fast. Stop by roadside stands
for grilled meat tacos and local sugar filled
fruit punch, a few words and wondering stares.
Night falls to find myself driving
young hippie girl her hair and breast
soft against my shoulder asleep,
fighting off tired eyes to stay alive,
fighting off the lust of her form to stay fit.
The morning breaks like a found lost memento,
breakfast of beans, tortillas and rice, spicy pepper
sauce in southern Oaxaca market, piles of peppers and mangos,
big city bustle as we eat in awe.
The owner asks if we have seen El Tule,
the world's largest tree. The words sting echo call to
some place unknown. A wanting place
needing of some sense. El Tule surely would so teach.
Only two hours north, barely off our path,
we head in silence towards visions of El Tule
that grip the mind like spiked cleats on grass.
We arrive, met by peddlers of key chains, mugs, ashtrays.
My bowels forbid exit, my feet override.
Pass more vendors, soda pop, hot dogs, hamburgers.
Littered ground like after new year's parade.
In front, El Tule surrounded by chain-link fence,
carved in graffiti, lovers' names immortal.
Photographers snap Polaroids for tourists who barely look

into the huge twisted branches, or the lonely magnificent girth
untouched
protected from those who seek to conquer, who will
ride to the next star on their map,
capture a photo and continue on equally untouched.

Mummies

The museum is behind the hill from where they
pull the dead, that now rest not so gently, or are sold as images
in trinkets and toys to be treasure chest lost, or as delectable

syrupy brown sugar candies, texture like cobwebs,
molded into delicious mummies,
sombreros, wrapped in sarapes, the colors of the

Mexican flag. Covered in plastic, gripped in pleading hands,
the hawkers fight for our attention, dismiss each other,
nearly come to blows for the dwindling pesos.

These vendors, soon enough, buried in the fields where the mummies grow.
If they rot ever so gently, the perfect one out of twenty,
they will eventually rest in glass cases naked for photo snapping masses.

Six mummies for thirty pesos, the best mummy
candy in town. The Chinaman, the doctor,
for free the fat baby and the pregnant women.

Mummy skull bottle openers,
a mug that reads: I am DYING for a drink and a woman.
Fetus skull T-shirt, the name of the town underneath.

What of the souls of the dead, we ask?
What do we care of souls, they laugh hard,
what good are souls when it is food and drink we need?

Credits

Many of these poems have been previously published in the following magazines, journals, and anthologies: *Colere, Steel Point Quarterly, MiPo, Free Lunch, Haz Mat Review, Gawd is a Gangster, Fluid Ink Press, Branches, Standards: The Journal of Multicultural Studies, Another Sun, Verve, Wild Velvet, Ascent, Poor Mojo's Almanac, Nasty, Sugar Mule, Hinge, ZeeBook Zine, Whimperbang, Junket, Perigee, Tryst, Tahoma West,* and *The Sidewalk's End.*

Author Biography

Rich Furman, MFA, MSW, PhD, is the author or editor of over fifteen books, including a collection of flash nonfiction/prose poems, *Compañero* (Main Street Rag, 2007). Other books include *The Immigrant Other: Global and Transnational Issues* (Oxford University Press, 2016), *Social Work Practice with Men at Risk* (Columbia University Press, 2010), and *Practical Tips for Publishing Scholarly Articles* (Oxford University Press, 2012). His work has been published in *Another Chicago Magazine, Bluestem, Chiron Review, Sweet, Hawai'i Review, Pearl, Coe Review, The Evergreen Review, Black Bear Review, Red Rock Review, Sierra Nevada Review, New Hampshire Review, Penn Review*, and many others. He is Professor of Social Work at the University of Washington Tacoma. A qualitative researcher whose work is situated on the boundary between the expressive arts and the social sciences, he is one of the pioneers of poetic inquiry. He received his MFA in creative nonfiction from Queens University of Charlotte's MFA-Latin America program. He is, or has been in former incarnations, a punk, dishwasher, laminator, photographer, dad, social worker, busboy, chemical-spill cleaner, telemarketer, Time/Life bookseller, dance club bouncer, and dog petter. Petting dogs is what he does, and enjoys, best.